Bethlehem's Redeemer
Seeing Jesus in Ruth

A Learner's Workbook & Journal

Daniel J. Palmer

Learner's Guide Compiled and Edited by:
John M. Lewis

College&Clayton Press

ATHENS, GEORGIA

College&Clayton Press

Scripture quotations taken from the New American Standard Bible® (NASB). Copyright © 1960, 1962, 1963, 1968, 1971, 1972, 1973, 1975, 1977, 1995 by The Lockman Foundation. Used by permission. www.Lockman.org.

Bethlehem's Redeemer Learner's Workbook and Journal: Seeing Jesus in Ruth
Copyright © 2020 College and Clayton Press, LLC.
All Rights Reserved.

Based on *Bethlehem's Redeemer: Seeing Jesus in Ruth* Copyright © 2020 Daniel J. Palmer. All rights reserved. No part of this publication may be used or reproduced in any manner whatsoever without written permission unless such quotation is covered by fair use. For information, contact College and Clayton Press, LLC., PO Box 5533, Athens, GA 30604.

College and Clayton Press website: https://collegeandclayton.com

Cover Design: Daniel Blake Hulsey

ISBN: 978-1-7341915-5-4

Printed in the United States of America

Table of Contents

Editor's Preface ix

Introduction 1

Ruth One
No Bread in Bethlehem 15

Ruth Two
The Redeemer Who Gives Bread............................... 33

Ruth Three
The Redeemer is a Worthy Relative 53

Ruth Four
The Redeemer Willingly Pays a Price 71

Editor's Preface

This workbook is designed for readers to dig deeper into the book of Ruth and *Bethlehem's Redeemer: Seeing Jesus in Ruth*. Each chapter asks questions based on Daniel Palmer's book, the text of Ruth, and reflections on how the truths held in Ruth are demonstrated in your own life. Each chapter ends with space to journal through your study of Ruth with possible journaling prompts that you can use or simply us the space to contain your thoughts on what the Spirit is teaching you as you study Ruth.

The workbook is intended to be used with *Bethlehem's Redeemer: Seeing Jesus in Ruth*. It could be used as a learner's guide during a small group. It would likely be best to have learners read the chapters and complete the workbooks at home. Then come together to discuss the answers in the workbook and share their notes in their journal. The workbook and journal is also well suited for individuals who want to study on their own.

Whichever style works best for your situation, we hope you enjoy the depth of study this workbook will add to your time examining the Messianic content in the book of Ruth through Daniel Palmer's *Bethlehem's Redeemer*.

Introduction

The Book of Ruth opens with these words, "Now it came about in the days when the judges governed, that there was a famine in the land" (1:1a). The period of judges was marked largely by a neglect of God's Word and, with some notable exceptions, judges who lost sight of the privilege of serving God and leading His people. Judges concludes with these sobering words, "In those days there was no king in Israel; everyone did what was right in his own eyes" (Judges 21:25).

The concluding thought in Judges is that God's people need a king who will guide them into God's truth – the king the Lord promised to provide through the house of Judah (Gen 49:8–12). The opening of Ruth does not sound like the beginning of a story that leads to the provision of God's forever king, but we should not be surprised that it is.

When God works at the height of human hopelessness, it puts an end to human boasting. Ruth, a book that begins with a famine and a family who leaves God's people for food among the people of Moab becomes a book that forms a bridge between a spiritual low point in Israel and the birth of David, "a man after God's own heart" (1 Sam 13:14) anointed King over God's people.

The book of Ruth ends with a natural segue into the life of David in 1 Samuel. As John Sailhamer writes, "The genealogy at the conclusion of the book makes the final link between this story and the birth of David—as well as the Son of David, the Messiah."[1] The significance of this observation is difficult to overstate. While Ruth is, according to Mary J. Evans, "an account, largely based on dialogue, of the life and concerns of one small Israelite family,"[2] it is not only that. To approach Ruth as a story of one family and a study in family, historical, and cultural dynamics, is to miss out on the book's primary message about God's coming promised Son and King.

My concern is that, whether it is Ruth, or most of the other Old Testament narratives, Christians often miss out on seeing the Son of God in the Old Testament.

The coming Son of God and God's unmerited gift of life in Him is the overarching theme and message of the Old Testament, and, as we will see, it is the story of Ruth. The church desperately needs to see Jesus as the subject of the Old Testament because, as Jesus says, "This is eternal life, that they may know You, the only true God, and Jesus Christ whom You have sent" (John 17:3). When the church consistently sees Jesus in the Old Testament:

> "When God works at the height of human hopelessness, it puts an end to human boasting."

- It increases her knowledge and understanding of Him and His work in the here and now.
- It enables her to better understand the New Testament.
- It strengthens her faith in Him.
- It deepens her love and appreciation and worship of the living Lord Jesus Christ, God's Son.

Introduction

The Book of Ruth recounts the story of a family that initially abandons the land of the Lord's promises and His people because of a famine. Yet, by the story's end, the family is miraculously redeemed when God provides a miracle son in Bethlehem. As we will see, there is more to the story, but that is the basic outline. A miracle son brings redemption to Naomi's family and includes a Gentile woman, Ruth the Moabitess, in this story of redemption and as a mother in the lineage of King David and, eventually, of Jesus, the King of Kings.

All of this happens in Bethlehem. During Advent, Micah 5:2 is frequently (and accurately) cited as a direct prophecy of Jesus's birth in Bethlehem. While Micah 5:2 is clear and direct evidence, Ruth also highlights God's plan to send His Promised Son to be born in Bethlehem. As we will see, by chapter four, Ruth connects the story of the provision of God's Promised Son from Abraham to Judah, to Boaz and Obed and all the way to King David. On a first reading of the Old Testament, it may not seem that Bethlehem figures all that prominently in the story of God's redemption through His Son, but the Book of Ruth suggests otherwise. In Ruth, Bethlehem of Judah is shown to stand at the center of the story of the provision of many sons who are in the genealogical line leading to the birth of David in Bethlehem.

Ruth is a book that helps us understand that in God's story what is most significant often happens in the narratives we tend to overlook. Ruth, just a few pages in the Old Testament, connects so much of what God is doing for and through His people in the world. What happens in Bethlehem must not be overlooked; indeed, it is essential to the story the redemption of God's people. Without God's provision of a son in the house of bread (i.e. Bethlehem), the people of God would have no king in the city of peace (i.e. Jerusalem). This was true in the journey from the period of the Judges to the rise of

King David, and it would be true again when it seemed God's promises of a forever King in the line of David had failed. Long after David has died, the story of Ruth beckons us to remember what God accomplished in Bethlehem, trusting that if David had come from a family line that was as good as dead, the Promised Son would surely come, and He would come from Bethlehem.

> "In God's story what is most significant often happens in the narratives we tend to overlook."

As we recognize that the seemingly obscure town of Bethlehem is central to God's story of redemption, the Spirit begins to open our eyes to see that other details in Ruth are guideposts helping us to recognize Jesus as God's ultimate redeemer. The truth that God's redeeming son comes "from Bethlehem" is only the beginning of what God reveals in Ruth.

Ruth not only highlights the location for the arrival of God's Redeeming Son; it also reveals the Son Himself. The Old Testament speaks about Jesus not only through direct prophecies but in the details of the stories about the featured sons of promise who are highlighted along the way to the Son of Promise. It is not accidental that Ruth is a story of a miraculous redemption through the birth of a son in Bethlehem.

Ruth is preparing us to recognize Jesus, God's Promised Son and Redeemer, who is miraculously conceived in the Virgin Mary and born in Bethlehem. Ruth is more than a short story about one family's redemption; it is a Spirit-authored story about Jesus, God's Son of Promise – a story that reveals not only where God's redeemer will be born (i.e. Bethlehem) but also who Jesus is as God's ultimate redeeming Son.

In chapter 1, we will see that redemption begins when we stop seeking our own "bread" in enemy territory and instead turn to the

Lord. In chapter 2, we will see that access to the bread God provides in Bethlehem must come through a son who will graciously provide it. As Boaz welcomes Ruth to work in his field and graciously provides for her needs and the needs of Naomi, we see a picture of Jesus who welcomes Gentiles into the family of God by offering Himself to them as the bread of life. In chapter 3, as Boaz faces great temptation on the threshing floor, we see a picture of Jesus who is a worthy man, a man who refused to yield to temptation so that sinners may be redeemed from sin. The need for a redeemer who is a close relative also comes into view, as we see that the incarnation of Jesus was necessary for Him to be a "near relative" or "kinsman redeemer" for sinners. In chapter 4, multiple aspects of redemption are beautifully brought together. The refusal of another possible kinsman redeemer demonstrates that redemption is costly, and Jesus willingly pays the price. Boaz's marriage to Ruth illustrates the intimacy of redemption in Jesus, a redemption in which He marries Himself to the church by sacrificing Himself for her good. The miraculous conception of Obed in the womb of a barren, Gentile widow helps us understand Jesus is, indeed, a son and a Savior for people from all nations. The birth of Obed in the place of Elimelech and his sons demonstrates Jesus will be a son who is born to take the place of sinners so that those who would otherwise remain dead in their trespasses and sins might be raised up to life everlasting in God's land. Finally, the concluding genealogy reminds us God's story has always been about how God keeps His promises through His Son, a Son who would rule as King. Jesus is in the text of Ruth; let's go see Him and feast upon Him there (John 6:41ff).

Endnotes

1. John H. Sailhamer, *The Books of the Bible*, (Grand Rapids: Zondervan, 1998), 25.
2. Mary J. Evans, *Judges and Ruth*, The Tyndale Old Testament Commentaries (Downers Grove, IL: Inter-Varsity Press, 2017), 239.

Journal

Possible Prompts:
- Have you ever explicitly reflected on your "process" for interpreting the Bible?
- How have you seen the gospel of the promised Son in the Old Testament in general or in another Old Testament book?
- What questions do you have at the beginning of this exploration that seeks the gospel of Jesus in the book of Ruth?

Introduction 7

Introduction

Introduction

Introduction

Ruth One
No Bread in Bethlehem

As we read Ruth 1, we encounter a woman, Naomi, who fled to Bethlehem during a famine, now encouraging her two widowed and childless daughters-in-law to remain in their homeland of Moab as she returns to Bethlehem. Naomi's reason for urging them to stay behind catches our attention—it is impossible for her to give them sons to marry and care for them. Furthermore, their lack of children suggests they been unable to conceive (vv. 11–13). It seemed best to Naomi that Orpah and Ruth stay behind in Moab and do what they could to provide for themselves among their own people in familiar territory. If they return with her, their only hope would be that the Lord would do the impossible and provide a son in Bethlehem in the place of Elimelech and his sons to give them life, provision, and standing in their new home and among a new people.

Ruth opens with a critical and life-defining choice that will only lead to sustained blessing if God provides a son in Bethlehem. We know, because Ruth ends with the birth of a son who is in the line of Judah and a forefather of King David and of King Jesus, that God does provide such a son, but we do not know that yet. Before we arrive there, we must first consider chapter 1, a story of repentance that sets in motion God's eventual provision through the birth of an unlikely son.

Scene One: Flight, Famine and Futility | God Wants Us to Turn to Him (vv. 1–5).

We could call the first scene (vv. 1–5), flight, famine, and futility. The major theme in this opening scene runs throughout the Scripture and is foundational to our understanding and presentation of the gospel. To be rescued by God, we must turn not to ourselves but to the Lord as King.

1. What is the foundational theme of Ruth 1? (p. 35-36)

2. Why is there a famine in the land? How might Deut. 8:11-14 relate to the famine? (p. 36)

3. Should Elimelech have fled the Promised Land for Moab? Why or why not?

4. How might Elimelech fleeing to Moab be different than Joseph bringing his family to Egypt in the midst of famine?

5. How do trials expose our faith as lacking? How do trials refine our faith? How can Christians see trials as a source of joy? Is there a trial you have gone through that you can look back on in joy? Is there a current trial you are in that you see with joy?

6. Describe Moab's relationship with Israel. (p. 40)

7. Should Mahlon and Chilion have married women from Moab? Why or why not?

8. How does the parable of the prodigal son relate to Ruth 1? (p. 41)

9. How did Naomi's life come into jeopardy? What was the solution for this danger? (p. 41-42)

Scene Two: Decision Time | To turn to God, we must trust Him to provide for us against all odds (vv. 6–19a).

In verse 6, we have a sliver of hope, a light shining in the darkness. Naomi has no son, but she learns Yahweh has "visited" His people. He has cared for them by providing "food." The activity of God is evident throughout Ruth. Verse 6 is one of two places in Ruth where God is specifically said to act. God broke the famine in Bethlehem for the sake of His people. There was food (literally, "bread") again in the House of Bread.

10. Is Ruth's assessment of her situation correct in Ruth 1:13? Did God move against Ruth, or did Ruth abandon God?

11. Ruth becomes hopeless. How should we respond when we become hopeless? Is there a time when you have felt hopeless? What pulled you out of it?

12. How is Ruth 1 about a "turn" or "return?" (p. 44)

13. What does the Hebrew word *hesed* mean? How is it used in Ruth 1? (p.46)

14. How do Orpah and Ruth's responses to Naomi's statements in Ruth 1 demonstrate worldly and godly sorrow? Can you think of an example of Godly sorrow from history or your own life? (p. 48)

15. Describe Ruth's profession of faith in vv. 16–17.

16. Elimelech and his family were disobedient to God. God did not require this disobedience, but He acted faithfully in spite of this disobedience. How have we seen God act faithfully even in the midst of Elimelech and Naomi's disobedience?

Scene Three: Entering Bethlehem | When those who are empty turn to the Lord, God gives a harvest (vv. 19b–22).

Naomi returns to Bethlehem, and it stirs up "all the city" (v. 19). Naomi had been away from the people of God and the place of God's provision for at least a decade and likely longer. She had left for a sojourn that ended up severing her from God's people and His provision. Long before she had been short on physical bread, she had been missing out on knowing and trusting God her provider.

17. What does Naomi change her name to? What does Naomi's new name mean? What is significant about this name change? (p. 50)

18. How does "Act 1" end?

19. How has Ruth 1 pointed towards the Son of God?

To understand how God will provide for Naomi and Ruth, we must keep reading, but for now, we trust the implicit promise of v. 22; it is the beginning of barley harvest, and God finishes what He starts (Phil 1:6).

We know God finishes what He starts because He sent His Son who declared from the cross, "It is finished" (John 19:30). God sent His Son to a world starved for His presence because of their sin. This Son would be broken to forgive our sins and to fill us, not with mere bread, but with life everlasting in Himself. It is no accident that Jesus, the Bread of Life, is born in Bethlehem, the House of Bread. All the hope and promise of Ruth is fulfilled when the promised Son of God who brings ultimate redemption and deliverance to God's people comes. God does provide a Son, and He is our daily bread. In Jesus, we have the "bread" which truly satisfies. This is why, centuries after this story, Mary, while anticipating the birth of Jesus, declares "[The Lord] has filled the hungry with good things" (Luke 1:53).

If you are hungry, leave your sinful self-reliance and stubborn insistence on your own way behind, and turn to the Lord. Jesus was born in Bethlehem to die for your sins and to be raised to give you a new life in Him. If you are empty, come to Jesus and be filled. The bread you really need comes from Bethlehem.

Journal

Possible Prompts:
- What have you learned about Jesus in Ruth 2?
- Reflect on the last paragraph regarding our emptiness and sin and the salvation Jesus offers.
- You could reflect further on how trials have refined you and your relationship with God.
- Are there other ways the gospel is reflected in Ruth 1 other than those mentioned in this chapter?

Ruth 1

Ruth Two
The Redeemer Who Gives Bread

In chapter 1, we saw the story of a family who fled Bethlehem and the land of God's people to pursue provisions in Moab. Rather than take refuge in the Lord, they left for a quick fix, abandoning the people and place of God's promises and everlasting provision to come through His Son (Psalm 2:12). Though they lived in Bethlehem and were of the tribe of Judah from which God had promised a forever-King (Gen 49:8–10), they left. After a decade (or perhaps more) in Moab, Naomi has found physical bread, but she has not found the "abundant life" that comes to those who trust God will provide for His people through His promised Son (John 10:10). Her experience is "bitter" because her husband and two sons die, leaving her childless (1:6).

Ruth 1 demonstrates we need more than mere bread to have true life. As Jesus says, "Man shall not live on bread alone, but on every word that proceeds out of the mouth of God.'" (Matt 4:4; cf Deut 8:3). We do not just need bread; we need bread on God's terms.

Even after Naomi hears of bread in Bethlehem, she has little reason to return other than that she is finally hungry for more than mere bread. She is turning to the Lord and His promises. If He can bring bread back to Bethlehem, perhaps He will overcome the bitterness of life she has encountered since abandoning Him.

In strictly human terms, Naomi has no reason to return. She has no husband to provide for her and no sons to continue the family name or secure her property rights. She does not even have a consistent and reliable source of daily bread.

Though faced with seemingly insurmountable odds, Naomi returns. Ruth, one of her widowed, Moabitess daughters-in-law (v. 2) follows her to Bethlehem, and this book ends up bearing her name. The other daughter-in-law, Orpah, does not follow Naomi, and she never again appears in God's story. Ruth is showing us that turning to the Lord and His people makes a forever-difference in whether you have a forever-place in God's story. Chapter 2 begins to show us how God brings His redemption to those who turn to Him.

When Naomi and Ruth arrive in Bethlehem, "it is the beginning of barley harvest" (1:22). The Lord gives bread to His people in Bethlehem, but how Naomi or Ruth will access the Lord's provision remains to be seen. Chapter 1 leaves us with the question of how Naomi and Ruth will survive and have a standing in the land without a husband or a son. How will the good news of bread in Bethlehem become good news for these two widows who have no reliable access to the bread God is providing?

> "We do not just need bread; we need bread on God's terms."

Scene 1: Ruth happens upon Boaz's field | We must recognize our need for God's grace (vv. 1–3)

Verse 1 is packed with information about this man God uses to redeem both Ruth and Naomi. How that happens remains to be seen,

Ruth 2

but to understand chapter 2, we need to realize the Spirit is beginning to paint a picture through Boaz of God's Promised Son—the ultimate redeemer who comes from Bethlehem. The language of verse 1 helps us arrive at this conclusion.

1. What three ways can *gibbor* be taken? How does Boaz fit into each of these descriptions? (p. 57-58)

2. How do Psalm 45 and Leviticus 25:25 contribute to our understanding of *gibbor*? (p. 58-59)

   a) Psalm 45:

b) Leviticus 25:25:

3. What is gleaning? How does it relate to Christian charity? How can individuals, churches, and governments implement a notion of gleaning? (p. 59-60)

4. Ruth and Naomi had long term and short term needs. Ultimately, their long term needs were redemption. But their immediate need was food or bread and sustenance. How do we balance these two types of needs in ministries in our church and our community? What are ways you are gifted to meet immediate needs of others around you?

Ruth 2

Scene 2: Meeting Boaz | We must behold God's redeemer and receive His bread (vv. 4-16)

Verse 4 opens with the words, "Now behold, Boaz" or "Look, Boaz!" The reader of the story finally meets the character verse 1 anticipates, and we are asked to behold him. In both his identity as a near relative (spelled out in chapter 3) and in his initial actions in chapter 2, we behold not merely Boaz but a picture of God's Son the ultimate redeemer from Bethlehem. In beholding Boaz, we see the amazing grace God gives through this man and a picture of the grace to come in Christ.

As we consider Boaz's lavish provision for Ruth, we are reminded of Christ's even more lavish provision for us—fullness of joy in the presence of God, direct access to the Father through Him, forevermore. Let's behold Boaz!

5. How is Jesus the "greater Boaz?" (p. 63-65)

6. What are ways we need Jesus to be the "greater Boaz" in our own lives?

7. Who are people in your community or city that are marginalized? What needs do they have that you, your small group, or your church could meet?

8. Boaz's treatment of Ruth in calling her "daughter" and bringing her under the protection of his household demonstrates the radical nature of salvation. Think of people you feel are enemies to your way of life. Are these members of another religion,

another political party, another college affiliation? What would it look like to love them the way Boaz loves Ruth or Jesus loves us?

9. Boaz gives Ruth a new identity when he calls her daughter. Reflect on the parts of your past that are put to death that no longer have to be your identity now that you are in Christ. Are there things in your life now that steal away your identity from being in Christ?

10. How is Ruth 2:9 a picture of the gospel? (p. 68)

11. In the explanation of Ruth 2:8, we see a picture of Boaz limiting where Ruth gleans in a similar manner to how salvation is limited to interacting with the Son. How does the exclusivity of the gospel relate to loyalty to God and God's provision of salvation?(p. 68-69)

Ruth 2

12. How does Ruth respond to this provision in 2:10–13? (p. 69-70)

13. Why do we need rest and refuge from the LORD? What passages in the New Testament and Old Testament address these needs? In what areas of your life do you long to rest in Christ? What is an area of strife you long to take refuge in?

Scene 3: Ruth Shares with Naomi and Returns to the Harvest | We must share with others and reap until the harvest is complete (vv. 17–23)

Until verse 17, Ruth has been mostly passive in her action. She walks to the fields in hope, but it is Boaz who notices her, feeds her, and commissions her to work in his field with all the protection she will need to do so with confidence. Ruth's work begins after she receives God's gracious provision through Boaz. Her work is to harvest in Boaz's field, and the same is true for us. When Christ draws us near to feast upon Him, He does it not only to fill us but also to nourish us for the work of harvesting.

In verse 18, Ruth is again "satisfied" (see v. 14), and she has plenty left to share with Naomi. This is a picture of how God provides for us in Christ. In the miracle of the feeding of the 5,000, Jesus multiplies the bread and they "all ate and were satisfied" (Mark 6:42). In the miracle of the feeding of the 4,000, Jesus uses the disciples to distribute the bread, and the bread just keeps on coming. Seven loaves become enough bread for 4,000 with leftovers. Ruth is showing us that true satisfaction comes from a redeemer who is able to keep supplying us with nourishment we can give away and lose nothing in the process.

14. How does Boaz's provision for Ruth exceed her need? How does this same type of thing happen for us spiritually with Christ? How do we translate this into being Christlike in our own lives? (p. 74)

Ruth 2

15. How does is God's *hesed* revealed in Ruth 2 (esp. 2:20)? How is God's kindness transforming Naomi? (p. 75-76)

Boaz's provision, like the provision of Jesus, comes to those who are enlisted as laborers in his field. Redemption is not merely for us but for others as well. Those who are redeemed by the Redeemer from Bethlehem are those who willingly and eagerly keep returning to the Redeemer's field to participate in his harvest.

> "When Christ draws us near to feast upon Him, He does it not only to fill us but also to nourish us for the work of harvesting."

Ruth, for her part, is ready to go back noting that Boaz had given her permission to remain with his servants until "they have finished all my harvest." Naomi, perhaps hoping for an opportunity for Ruth to marry Boaz, urges Ruth to stay close to Boaz's maids and not to his male servants. However, as we close chapter 2, the emphasis is on Ruth's continued work as a full partner in the work of the harvest. Ruth accepts Boaz's proposal, working in his harvest and remaining with Naomi.

This is a picture of what happens in the life of one who is redeemed by Christ. When we really taste of Christ and see that He is good, we continue to feast upon Him not by keeping Him to ourselves but in sharing Him with others.

16. How do we participate in Christ's "redeeming harvest?"

_____

_____

_____

_____

_____

_____

If Christ has redeemed you, you have been redeemed to embody Christ's compassion for those who still need to hear of Him and trust Him. He has saved you to send you into His field, and He does not send you alone. He sends you as a part of His church, His servants, people who "stay close" (v. 21) to one another and support one another in our Redeemer's field until the harvest is done.

May God find us faithful to feast upon Christ our Redeemer. May we regard ourselves as a bunch of undeserving outsiders filled up to overflowing by God's miraculous provision for our lives in Christ, and may He find us eager to share His Promised Son and Redeemer with others, reaping in His harvest until the harvest is finished.

Journal

Possible Prompts:
- What have you learned about Jesus in Ruth 2?
- Reflect further on our proper response to God's provision in Jesus.
- Reflect on how God's *hesed* or "loving kindness has transformed you.
- Are there other ways the gospel is reflected in Ruth 2 other than those mentioned in this chapter?

Ruth 2

Ruth 2

Ruth Three
The Redeemer is a Worthy Relative

In chapter 2, Ruth goes out to glean, and God gives her what she prays for (v. 2:2)—one who takes notice of her and shows her incredible kindness (*hesed*, 2:20). Boaz does not merely allow Ruth to pick grain in his field. He offers protection. He gives her bread and vinegar before sending her out into his field to harvest. He tells her to stay only in his field and allows her to gather all the way to the end of the barley and wheat harvests. When Ruth reaps in Boaz's field, she is satisfied, and she has more than enough to share with Naomi.

By the end of chapter 2, our confidence is growing that God is using Boaz to give us a picture of the lavish redemption He ultimately bestows upon His people through the gift of Jesus, His Promised Son. God the Son left heaven to be conceived in Mary, born in Bethlehem, and given the name Jesus. He came to do what His name suggests, which is to grant salvation—in the language of Ruth, redemption. He came to pay for sins and be raised up to a forever-life through which all who trust in Him may know the satisfaction that can only come to those who know Him as the Bread of Life.

For Ruth and Naomi to be redeemed, they need Boaz more than they need Boaz's bread. For Naomi to be rescued, an animal or an angel will not do. She must have a son to carry on the family name and inheritance in the land. There must be someone related to her husband who will pay the price to redeem her land and give her, a woman too old to have a child, a son. What is needed is God's provision of a miracle son to take the place of her dead sons—a son who will redeem.

> "To be redeemed by the Lord, we must first know the emptiness of self-reliance."

Boaz seems to be a possible solution. But the harvest seasons are ending, and nothing has happened. Naomi grows impatient and devises a plan to at least help Ruth. As a result, we get a look at the character of Bethlehem's Redeemer.

Scene 1: The plans of an impatient mother-in-law | The faithful should wait upon the Lord (vv. 1–6)

In chapter 1, we saw Naomi's repentance in her return to Bethlehem. We also saw her confession that she was pleasant when she was full of herself and had a full house, but when God emptied her, she was bitter. She was starting over in Bethlehem with only the Lord. She was exactly where we must be to know and enjoy the wonder of being filled by the Lord. To be redeemed by the Lord, we must first know the emptiness of self-reliance.

Now, as we saw in chapter 2, Naomi has been filled. In accordance with God's Word, Ruth went out to glean. She happened upon Boaz's field, and both Ruth and Naomi were filled because of God's lovingkindness to them through Boaz (v. 2:18).

> "For all who will stop their striving, planning, and scheming and come to Jesus, we can rest."

Ruth 3

However, after she has been graciously filled, Naomi returns to making plans to provide for herself. God is already proving He will provide, but Naomi decides to try to speed things along.

1. How did self-reliance cause issues for Naomi? What ways do we replace trust in God's faithfulness with self-reliance? How do we guard against apathy or inaction in attempts to be reliant on Christ?

2. Naomi's desires for Ruth are good. Naomi's means are morally compromising. How do you combat temptations to secure a good end through bad means? What are areas in your life or past where this has come up?

3. Naomi wants her will to be God's will, but she fails to wait on God. What are times in your life where you tried to shove your plans or goals ahead of God's timing? What is a time in your life where you waited on God? What was the difference?

Scene 2: Boaz is tested | The redeemer from Bethlehem redeems in God's way (vv. 7–15)

In verse 7, we read that Ruth came to Boaz "secretly," likely concealing her identity with the shawl (v. 15) she would soon use to carry home six measures of barley to Naomi. The secrecy adds to the suspense. Deeds done in secret are no secret to God. As Ecclesiastes 12:14 says, "For God will bring every act to judgment, everything which is hidden, whether it is good or evil." Boaz is facing a most serious test. He has a full stomach. He has worked hard at the threshing floor, and he has lain down in the pitch-black countryside outside Bethlehem. In this modern era, it is difficult to conceive of the darkness that would have characterized the rural countryside in the fields surrounding the town of Bethlehem. This is can't-see-your-hand-in-front-of-your-face darkness. Verse 8 says it is "the middle of the night." The crisis and climax of this story has come under the cover of darkness.

Ruth 3

4. What is significant about Boaz working late at the threshing room? (p. 87, 89)

5. Sex is designed by God to be a unitive and procreative action that blesses marriage with emotional connectivity and children who will honor their parents and the Lord. Since the Fall, sex has been constantly misused. We are all guilty of some misuse of God's design for sex at some point in our lives. Boaz rises to the occasion in this moment. What does Boaz do right? What advice do you give to others (and yourself) to avoid misusing sex?

6. How does Boaz's treatment of Ruth at the threshing floor look forward towards Christ's character as a redeemer? (p. 91)

7. What is significant about Ruth's request for Boaz to spread his covering over her? (p. 91)

8. How does the story of Ruth demonstrate God's desire for all the nations to come to Him? (p. 91-92)

9. What is a kinsman-redeemer? (p. 92-94)

10. What is redemption? Why are people incapable of redeeming themselves? (p. 93)

11. How is Jesus our kinsman-redeemer? What role does seeing Christ as a groom play in our understanding of Jesus as the kinsman-redeemer? (p. 95)

12. How is the phrase "woman of excellence" used in the OT? How is this rare phrase applied to Ruth? How does this rare phrase apply to the Church? (p. 96-97)

Scene 3: Waiting for the Resolution | We must wait on the Lord and trust the Redeemer will act on behalf of those who come to Him (vv. 16–18)

In verse 16, Naomi does not ask Ruth, "How did it go?" but, literally, "Who are you?" It is the same question Boaz asked when he was startled awake at the threshing floor (v. 8). Naomi wants to know if she is Ruth as she has known her or Ruth as a woman betrothed to Boaz. Being married, or united, to the redeemer from Bethlehem is ultimately an issue of identity. When Ruth marries Boaz, she will forever be different.

13. In v. 16, how is Naomi's question "Who are you?" related to our identity in Christ? (p. 101)

14. How does scene three, build upon our understanding of salvation and redemption from scene two?

Ruth 3

15. In Ruth 3, how is Naomi different from the beginning of the chapter (scene 1) compared to the end (scene 3)? (p. 101)

The promise of the gospel according to Ruth is that there is rest and security and provision under the wing of God's redeemer from Bethlehem. For all who will stop their striving, planning, and scheming and come to Jesus, we can rest. Jesus is the kinsman redeemer from Bethlehem who left heaven to assume our humanity and do all that was necessary for the emptiness of our sin and scheming to be replaced with the fullness of life that is available in Him. Cease your striving. Sit down. Trust in Jesus, the redeemer from Bethlehem.

Journal

Possible Prompts:
- What have you learned about Jesus in Ruth 3?
- Do you ever find it hard to accept that God's provision might not work out exactly as you planned or accepted?
- Are there other ways the gospel is reflected in Ruth 3 other than those mentioned in this chapter?

Ruth 3

Ruth 3

Ruth Four
The Redeemer Willingly Pays a Price

Chapter 3 closes with Naomi expressing confidence that Boaz will prove to be a man who lives up to his name. Boaz means quickness or strength, and she believes Boaz "will not rest until he has settled [the issue of redeeming Ruth and Naomi] today" (3:18). She expects strong and decisive action from Boaz. Chapter 4 will prove whether or not Boaz is the sort of redeemer we have hoped. Is he all talk and show until the time for costly action comes, or is he really a worthy man who will redeem?

Scene 1: "Boaz Deals at the City Gate" | We must see that redemption is costly (vv. 1–8)2

When chapter 4 opens, Boaz is no longer at the threshing floor. He is at the town's gate. Boaz is not a procrastinator, and the shift in setting is designed to help us internalize the swiftness of Boaz's action.

1. Why do you think Boaz has the elders come sit to observe the conversation with the other possible kinsman-redeemer? (p. 108-109)

2. How does Boaz show us something about Jesus in Ruth 4:1–8? (p. 110)

3. Why does the other kinsman refuse to redeem Naomi and Ruth? (p. 110-111)

4. What does the introduction of the other kinsman teach us about redemption? (p. 111)

Ruth 4

In the Old Testament, the costliness of redemption is featured prominently.

5. How does God redeem Israel from slavery in the Exodus? (p. 111-112)

The ongoing requirement of a redemption price for the firstborn sons of Israel suggests there is a need for a firstborn son of Israel to die for full and final redemption (not merely from physical slavery but slavery to sin and death) to be accomplished. There have been clues about this from before the time of the Passover.

6. How is the OT theme of the Promised Son demonstrated in Genesis? (p. 112)

True redemption will require more than the blood of lambs or the payment of shekels; it will require the death of a worthy, firstborn son of Israel. He will be a son who is willing to pay whatever price is necessary to end the curse of death and raise up to a whole new way of life all the sons and daughters He redeems. The author of Ruth highlights the price of Naomi's redemption because it is a picture of the costliness of our redemption.

Scene 2: Marriage and Redemption | We must see that redemption comes when a qualified redeemer willingly pays the price of redemption, unites himself with the redeemed, and gives his Son to raise the sons of men (vv. 9–16).

In verses 9–10, Boaz does what he promised to do. He pays the price Mr. So-and-So would not pay. Boaz shows that God holds nothing back from those He rescues when He redeems.

7. How is Naomi in Moab a portrait of human separation from God? How did the death of Naomi's sons lead to her salvation? (p. 114)

8. What do the elders mean when they bless Ruth by saying they hope she is like Rachel and Leah? (p. 115)

Ruth 4

9. How does Jesus fulfill the elders blessing that Boaz will have enduring wealth and fame? (p. 116)

10. What were the elders of Israel hoping for in this marriage between Boaz and Ruth? (p. 116)

11. How does the Lord demonstrate His continued faithfulness to Ruth and His covenant with Israel through Ruth's pregnancy with Obed?

12. How does Obed "serve" Naomi? (p. 117)

13. How is Jesus the "greater Obed?" (p.117-118)

14. What five things does redemption mean? (p. 118-121)

a)

b)

c)

d)

Ruth 4

15. What do Christians inherit from their redemption? (p. 118)

16. What is restored for Christians when they are redeemed? (p. 118)

17. How is redemption relational? (p. 119)

18. How is redemption about the fame of the Son? (p. 120)

19. How does the book of Ruth demonstrate redemption comes from a son who raises up that which is dead? (p. 121)

Scene 3: The Coming King | God saves His people by sending His King, and He uses us in the process (vv. 18–22).

Ruth begins with a reminder that this story occurred during the time of the judges, a time when there was no King in Israel. It ends with King David's royal genealogy. Eventually King David would emerge from this story. There would be times in David's own life and in those who followed him where it would seem God's promises had failed. Yet, here stands the story of Ruth, a story of God's unfailing kindness given through a worthy kinsman redeemer, a story of a son of Judah and a woman from Moab. God's redemptive work through Boaz and Obed served as a reminder that God would surely keep His promise and send a forever Son and King to redeem His people.

20. How is the emergence of King David in this story a key indicator that God will answer the prayers of His people? (p. 122)

21. When is a moment when you have seen God's faithfulness to answering the prayers of His people? Have you offered these types of prayers before? How did you respond to God's answer? Did you notice God's faithfulness?

22. How does David, like Boaz and Obed, point to the future Redeemer from Bethlehem? (p. 122)

23. How does the book of Ruth push us to respond to God differently than we might be living right now?

24. God redeemed you for a purpose. That purpose may be great or small in our own eyes, but God has us on mission in everyday circumstances, in our jobs, homes, and in places far and wide. How does Ruth challenge us to see our redemption as being a part of a bigger purpose?

Do not let your circumstances, whatever famine there may be in your life, drive you from a God who has already proven His faithfulness by sending His Son. Do not let the challenges you face be the ruler with which you measure God's faithfulness. Measure God's faithfulness by the full pardon for sin that is available through Jesus, the Promised Son of God, the Redeemer from Bethlehem.

One day, Jesus will return and vanquish the remaining enemies of God and His people. He will set this world aright. Until He comes, Jesus is at work in the world winning the nations through people who trust that God keeps His promises even through the greatest of trials. He is winning the nations by including them in His family—people like Naomi and Ruth—people like you and me.

When God redeems us, He does it for a purpose far greater than our own salvation (as great as that is!). He does it so we would point others to the famous Son of Promise from Bethlehem, the worthy Son who alone can redeem. If you are in God's family; if God has taken you out of the land of His enemies (i.e. Moab) and made you a child of God; if God has filled your barren life with the indwelling presence of the Spirit of His Son; if these things are true in your life, God wants to use you as He used Naomi and Ruth. He wants to use you to bring Jesus to the world.

> "Until He comes, Jesus is at work in the world winning the nations through people who trust that God keeps His promises even through the greatest of trials."

Journal

Possible Prompts:
- What have you learned about Jesus in Ruth 4?
- Name your challenges and pray over them that you can see that God has been faithful in Jesus despite them.
- Are there other ways the gospel is reflected in Ruth 4 than those mentioned in the above chapter?

Ruth 4

Ruth 4

Ruth 4

Also Available from
College&Clayton Press

In this six-week devotional for men, Field Thigpen draws upon his ministry experience counseling and mentoring others to speak to the heart of men's uncertainties about identity, leading, and serving others. This book is not simply for young Christians seeking to mature in their faith. Thigpen writes for people who have lived, suffered, and lost. *Walk Like A Man* pushes the reader to continue maturing spiritually despite setbacks. Thigpen speaks to people in broken circumstances and points them towards God's desire to restore peace in the midst of trials.

In this updated edition of *Why Psalm 23 Is Not About You: Reading Psalm 23 in Its Context*, Dr. Robert L. Cole reveals linguistic and thematic patterns in the Psalter that demonstrates a continuity of meaning from Psalm 1 through Psalm 24. Particular attention is given to the meaning of Psalm 23 and it's surrounding Psalms. Fans of canonical studies and lovers of the Psalter will enjoy this quick, but thought provoking read.

College&Clayton Press

ATHENS, GEORGIA

We are a publishing company dedicated to producing quality works in Christian history, theology, and biblical studies. Our goal is to help foster the love of God with the mind. We hope that such an endeavor will also lead to the love of neighbor. Our conviction is that the fruits of solid research and interpretation are more open, thoughtful, and generous individuals. Please visit our website for our upcoming titles and other articles explaining more about who we are.

COLLEGEANDCLAYTON.COM

HISTORY // THEOLOGY // BIBLE STUDY